REACH for the Sun

A story
by
Robert Conklin

Illustrations and Calligraphy
by
Robert Bowman

Simon and Schuster · New York

Published by Simon and Schuster
A division of Gulf & Western Corporation
Simon and Schuster Building
Rockefeller Center
1230 Avenue of the Americas
New York, New York 10020

Designed by Robert Bowman

Manufactured in the United States of America

2 3 4 5 6 7 8 9 10

Library of Congress Catalog Card Number 77-20338

ISBN 0-671-24936-3

to
J.C.

The human spirit was born to grow and stretch as the flower breaks through the ground and reaches for the sun...

REACH
FOR THE SUN

There was a young man who grew up in today's
world.

But before becoming a young man he was a boy.

And ahead of that he was a baby. It was then
they noticed that here, indeed, was an unusual
young life. For those in his presence seemed
moved to a peace and contentment that was
beyond description.

It was clear that this one would be set apart
from the many.

So he became known as Solo.

His mother made him feel good. She fed and held him close to her, breathed tender sounds in his ear, smiled, bathed, powdered, caressed, loved, and enjoyed him. He glowed with confidence and satisfaction.

Then Solo learned to walk and felt proud.

But life became confusingly different. He was spanked, made to do strange things, sent from the room, told he was bad and only received a little of the usual affection.

He spilled milk, ripped a shirt, broke a cup, jumped on the bed, trampled a flower and got scolded for all of these. And more.

He tried to catch a ball, fly a kite, capture a butterfly, throw a stone, run fast, thread a needle, make a paper airplane, climb a tree and did not do any of these very well.

Then it became time to start school.

So he went into the world puzzled, insecure, lacking the caring love that he had once known...

...and unaware that everyone started life pretty much the same way.

School was not such a likeable experience.

Solo saw himself as one of a small flock that was led, corrected, confined, and told what could be learned, said, and done. The time away from school was more pleasant. This was spent playing ball, walking in the woods, swimming, and sleeping outdoors sometimes.

But best of all were the moments beside the water, looking in wonder at the clouds, birds, trees, and flowers.

There his mother found him one time and said, "Solo, I've been searching all over for you. Why didn't you come home for your meal?"

"I was feeding that which was more important than the body," he replied.

It seemed like a strange response from a 12 year old boy.

111

The schooling continued.

There were words and numbers...languages, mathematics, history, government, science, wars, laws, and what was happening in lots of places.

Then it was finished.

But countless questions were still unanswered. He did not learn...why people were not kind to one another...what held stones of confusion, despair, and fear on the hearts of so many...the origin and substance of thoughts and ideas... where he came from and where he would go... about the strange forces that churned about in his mind...

Why did they not talk more of these things? Is life so mysterious it must be kept in hiding?

There was so much to know and understand.

Solo went to work, trying a variety of tasks. He liked working outdoors best. It left his mind free to wander about, dream, and try to know itself.

After moving around for several years he finally settled near the mountains in a seacoast village named Lagonda. Just strolling along the picturesque streets and beside the sea was pleasant and inspiring. This was the way Solo was passing the time one sunny afternoon. He sauntered down the sidewalk of crooked concrete blocks, their cracks bulging with crabgrass...past homes whose faces carried the aging by the damp bay winds...beside shaggy hedges...along a wooden fence planed by the sea spray...to a grass filled patch and a bench beside a gnarled old tree.

He sat down, relaxed, and let the peacefulness of the moment play hazily on the strings of the senses. Time passed. The sun started pulling the shade of dusk across the sky.

Everywhere was quiet; the shadows seemed to stretch out and extend across his mind. It was almost like being in a different place at another time.

Then suddenly—voices! Shouts and coarse laughter could be heard. There emerged a male silhouette in grayish white plodding along the narrow street. Across the shoulders were heavy wooden beams.

Solo arose and joined the faces that stared in morbid concern. They shuffled along until the cobblestoned surface became rocks, dirt, and a barren slope.

The figure stumbled and fell. Men with knives strapped to their waists closed in, seized the arms and legs and laid them on the rough hewn wood that was fastened together in a T-shaped cross.

One of the group grasped a hand, turned the palm up, and held it flat against the slivery wood. Another placed the point of a square iron spike against the wrist. With one crunching blow metal was driven through the skin and flesh pinning it to the wood.

There was a gasp of fear and shock. The bearded face was twisted with pain.

The act was repeated on the other arm. Then the feet.

The men were noisier now. They cursed and jostled, uttering caustic, jeering remarks.

And then the wooden frame was raised with the figure on it twisting, squirming, wrenched with pain as the full weight of the body pulled at the flesh around the nails.

The man's reflexes resisted. The muscles tightened lifting the tortured form into a position to survive, to gasp for precious bits of air. But within minutes the strength ebbed. The mutilated physique slumped forward surrendering itself to the horrible anguish and breathlessness of gradual strangulation.

Blood dripped from the wrists and feet. The beard was wet with sweat and tears. The eyes, swelled with agony, looked down at the tormentors.

The lips parted.

Words were formed, barely loud enough to be heard.

"Father, forgive them, for they know not what they do."

Solo closed both eyes, lowering his face to his hands, cheeks moist with tears.

All about now was a tired blackness broken only by the moon's half-circle showing dimly through veils of would-be clouds. Bony trees pointed out the stars. The air was still and cool.

A voice, unheard but still incredibly clear, came out of the vastness saying: "Know me, Solo. But know me as spirit. I was born a man, lived as a man, and died as a man that man may know his spiritual nature. Let what I said sink deeply into your heart that you may have understanding. Then look well, Solo, within the crevices of your soul and you will find that which I found in mine…the way, the truth, the meaning of life. Let my message not be lost to the future as it has to the present."

IV

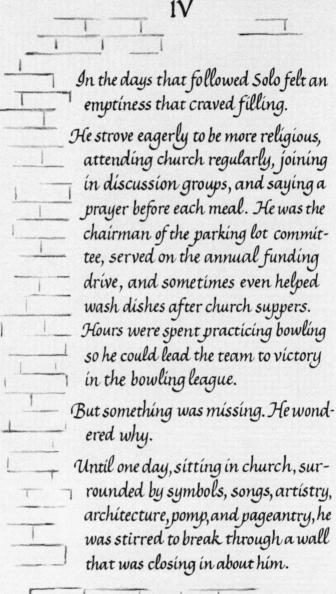

In the days that followed Solo felt an emptiness that craved filling.

He strove eagerly to be more religious, attending church regularly, joining in discussion groups, and saying a prayer before each meal. He was the chairman of the parking lot committee, served on the annual funding drive, and sometimes even helped wash dishes after church suppers. Hours were spent practicing bowling so he could lead the team to victory in the bowling league.

But something was missing. He wondered why.

Until one day, sitting in church, surrounded by symbols, songs, artistry, architecture, pomp, and pageantry, he was stirred to break through a wall that was closing in about him.

He left the building, went to the country, walked in the sunshine through the woods, and sensed the fresh green pushing through the faded coat of brown.

Tiny buds about to burst open clung to the bushes.

Insects hovered lazily in the streams of sunshine.

A faint breeze was trying to free a struggling feather from the twig that held it captive.

Birds were calling to each other.

Sitting there, surrounded by the sights and sounds of life, Solo's mind soared with celestial thoughts. He looked about and did not see the small as little, the large as big or that life had any size or separation at all. It was one.

He was an individualized expression of one life, one mind, one force, one power.

There came a mounting longing to look beyond that which could be understood and to start probing the unknown expanses that rested within. Such had been the human quest from the earliest worshipful scratchings on the cave walls. Invariably the searches had ended too soon, lulled into complacency by symbols, statues, words, or rituals. So the evolvement of the spiritual nature was shrouded and restrained.

The direction his life must take was now apparent.

V

A few days later Solo made his way into the mountains finally settling beside a stream. From there the valleys below and the mountain tops above could be seen.

There were aspen, larkspur, trout, dragon flies, sunshine and blue sky. The air was thin and fresh, warm in the day and cool at night.

Most of the time was spent fasting, in thought and meditation. There was temptation at times to yield to the cravings of the body, to give up the quest for truth. The humanness and intellect chattered that if the spirit within was supreme why not use it to bring pleasure to the body?

But there always came a stronger urge saying that human life does not live by food alone but by nourishment of a higher force. So he scoured the depths of consciousness to unlock doors that would lead to the ultimate awareness of life's meaning.

Little by little the ability to transcend into an exotic solitude high above the sensory functions was achieved. Finally, one day, in this exalted state of mind, Solo found that which merged with perfect oneness. From that moment the restlessness that had persisted was quieted. Instead was peace, a sense of union with the universal.

He had unravelled the meaning and mystery of life and, by so doing, became one of the spiritually enlightened to which the Divine Infinite reveals itself.

At last, the words of some time before were understood! "Know me, Solo. But know me as spirit. I was born a man, lived as a man, and died as a man that man may know his spiritual nature. Let what I said sink deeply into your heart that you may have understanding. Then look well, Solo, within the crevices of your soul and you will find that which I found in mine ...the way, the truth, the meaning of life. Let my message not be lost to the future as it has to the present."

He also became aware that the source for such words could not have been the Great Exception but, rather, the Great Example.

Solo wanted to stop the world and gather all people together to implant in them his wisdom and knowledge so the true state of their beings might become known. But, alas, most people would only resist and remain in darkness. For such awareness is a journey each must make alone.

All Solo could do was show the way.

About 40 days had gone past since the retreat in the mountains had begun. It was time, now, to leave.

VI

Arriving back at the village, Solo took up the new and uncharted pathway of his life, depending largely on intuition and revelation as guides.

People, about a dozen or so, whose minds were open, pliable and inquiring were selected. They were not especially wise nor scholarly but were good...and humble, representing the main stock of humanity.

Solo promised a greater adventure than they had ever known before. It would be a pursuit for truth and insight, an aroused revelation of each one's spiritual nature.

And so the pilgrimage began.

Solo talked to his People of many things.

"You are the individualized expression of that which is Perfect and Limitless," he said. "Your true self is spirit. It exists in you as it does in me. Seek it and you shall find it. The truth will be revealed and it will make you free. The way is easy. The reward is the comprehension of infinite life."

"But how shall we achieve such wisdom? Where shall we look?" they asked.

"Look within your own minds and hearts. Meditate. Contemplate on the words of those who have experienced spiritual enlightenment before you. But remember that is their occurrence, not yours. Heed mostly the illumination of your own soul, the voice that whispers within. That is the message of one who demonstrated this as the total experience of life. You are the dream of that which is perfect. Live so that you might fulfill that dream."

"Crave spiritual awakening. When you want to know the inner spirit as strongly as you want life you will find it and be renewed. And spend time in prayer."

"How shall we pray?" they asked.

He answered saying, "When you pray, do not do it openly to show others you are good. Be not as the hypocrites standing in the public gatherings. They say only words. They think they shall be heard for their much speaking. I say to you they have their rewards.

"Do not try to change God with prayers. Rather, let the prayers change you to receive the Power that knows your needs before they are uttered and is always waiting, loving, willing to flow into your hearts and minds.

"When praying go into a quiet place, alone,
and pray like this:

"Our Power which is in all,
Perfect is your being.
Your love has come,
Your will be done,
In body as it is in spirit.
Provide us this day with our daily needs,
And help us with our intolerances,
As we help those who are intolerant towards us;
And lead us not into false beliefs,
But deliver us from fear, doubt, and hate.
For yours is the One Mind, the One Power,
the One Spirit forever."

They followed this advice and gained a more penetrating perception of the unseen world of their true existence. They learned that there was no further to look than a blade of grass, a rising sun or their own miraculous minds and bodies in order to perceive the omnipotent Power that was directing life.

Channels of thought were opened removing the sediments of fear, doubt, guilt, and hate. Problems, joys, despairs, and hopes were shared. Talk was free and open, plumbing the depths of the inner selves.

They sat in quietness and deep meditation letting the invisible voice murmur to the hidden chambers of their souls. Every characteristic of the spiritual nature was pondered of which love was the most important.

They asked Solo about love and he answered: "When your heart sees all as one you will know love. Give it freely. Only by giving will you learn to love. For love is a growing, flourishing force that must be boundless, endless, and divisionless. It must be given without measure or reservation, even to those who do not return it. Love is the energy of life. It is the doorway to the unseen where truth, peace, joy and fulfillment exist."

As love became more meaningful the need for materialistic treasures faded and loosened them from the clutches of greed and envy.

VII

Time passed. Others were attracted to the simple doctrines directing the lives of this small group. The peace, joy, and love that resulted were quite apparent, also desperately needed in a civilization of turmoil, stress and confusion.

But with attention came rebuke. Solo and his People were condemned and accused of wanting to destroy religious foundations that had been constructed over the centuries. Solo denied this, saying, "I have no desire to break the traditions nor the cherished beliefs that have warmed the hearts and provided the guidelines for humanity. I want only to expand and fulfill them.

"Go with hungry souls and minds to your places of worship realizing that they are pathways not destinations. Your churches, shrines, temples and synagogues are the children of the spirit, not the parents."

But the words fell on deaf ears. Adversity mounted. For the world tends to isolate, fear, or avoid those in whom life has chosen to express itself differently. Newness, change, growth, and the unusual are viewed with alarm and resistance.

Yet how strange this is! For variations in other things are seen as delightful and inspiring. It is the mountain rising from the plain, and the waterfall breaking the monotony of the stream that are pleasing to the senses.

But what humanity sees in nature is not perceived in its own. It is irked and aggravated by any who deviate from the well worn ruts of culture, belief, or tradition.

And so as Solo's popularity rose so did the opposition. It looked as though the forces of resistance were, in fact, enflamed by his notoriety. The little movement for truth, beauty, and good would be seemingly burned out before it really got started.

How unfair! How unjust! Why wouldn't they listen? Why would they not at least find out what it was they were against before shaping their opinions?

Now Solo and his people were spending more of their time defending, justifying, and seeking mere acceptance than they were growing towards their ideals.

The rising resentment and hostility were beginning to tell on Solo. The zeal and vigor were slipping away ... replaced by listlessness and solitude. His People were concerned. This was not the man that once was. They pleaded with him to be examined by medical experts.

He finally agreed.

VIII

The verdicts were tragically the same...

...incurable...terminal...only a matter of time.

Solo was dismayed, bewildered. Although not afraid to die, he was confounded by the reason. Why? Why?

Was it a form of punishment? Or a burden to test the strength of faith?

Or maybe the skeptics were right. Life is just a physical experience that is piloted by fate and chance. No! No! It couldn't be! All that Solo was experiencing was diabolically contrary to the convictions that were so precious to him.

There was confusion and despair. And prayers.
Lots of them. In the darkness of night endless
moments were spent pondering, groping. Words
were sometimes hung in the heavy blackness...
"Why have you forsaken me?"

But time ticked on. The pleading petitions,
courageous thoughts, and determined struggles
were like trying to stop a rolling stone with a
feather. Little by little the reality of his condi-
tion chipped away at the strength of Solo's beliefs until there was little left to do with his
humanness except to abandon it to a greater
understanding.

That came about in the center of a night as he
was standing on a stretch of sand watching
the moonmist dance along the ripples of the sea.
Overhead was blackness polka-dotted with the
fluttering lights of the stars. It was still, vast
and beautiful.

In one blazing moment a unity was realized
with all that could be seen. Fired with joy
and excitement his words broke the quietness
of the night air : "My God and I are one!"

It was like a wind pushing aside the fog that
had engulfed his spirit. And with that he was
healed. The symptoms of distress might linger
on for a time but in his mind was the picture
that perfection was restored to the body.

Dropping to his knees in gratitude, words started rolling from one ear to the other. "I am free! I am well! Oh, my God! Thank you! My life! I have it back!"

And then a more solemn voice broke in: "It's so clear now! My anger and hostility lumped up within to cause my affliction. I had the freedom to set that aside at any time and seek truth. The words curable and incurable are inventions of the human mind. The magnificent loving power that heals knows of no such distinctions."

IX

The next morning Solo gathered his People together. The news of the recovery caused both jubilation and awe.

"It is a miracle!" they cried.

"No, quite the opposite," he replied. "It is the natural state of life. It is truth. It is the principle of all things. You have the freedom to do as I. Disease and misery are merely thistles on a floundering mind. Remove the thorns, let the mind seek its own, and life will be restored."

The people stood about, not saying much, wearing puzzled expressions on their faces.

Solo continued...

"You say you love, yet you sit in judgement of one another. You see the imperfections and differences in others. Your opinions turn inward and become burdens for your minds and bodies. I tell you, judge not lest you suffer likewise for your judgements.

"Life is spirit. It is endless, timeless and perfect. You talk of belief yet you doubt these words. So you fear death.

"The greatest tragedy of life is not death for that only alters the expression of life. Nor is sickness or poverty a greater calamity.

"The greatest tragedy of life is to inflict suffering on another; the next greatest is to do the same to yourselves.

"The light of the body is in the eye. If you look out at the world and see the truth, beauty and love of God, then your body will be filled with its likeness. But if your eye sees evil then your body and affairs will give way to what is seen.

"Seek first the kingdom of your spirit and all other things will follow."

They talked much of a new found power that was sensed as a regenerating force. Time passed swiftly that day as it did the next ...and the next.

Solo's presence now had a cleansing influence on men, women, and children. Human beings appeared to him as pure, unblemished spirit. His love and perception were so intense that those about him became the unconquerable images of his consciousness. Sickness, sin, and hopelessness fell from them as dried leaves from a tree. Many came from far and near to be healed and witness the wonders that were being done.

Solo's fame spread. Many looked upon him as having special powers and earthlessness.

"It is not I, but the Spirit within me that does these works," he would say. "You have the same within you. Believe that, have faith, and you will do even greater works than I."

These were not the words of one who wanted to enchain others. Here were promises of freedom from false beliefs, fear, and darkness. To many it was news of explosive gladness, a rebirth into a life few had dared to hope for.

But to others the acts of this man aroused resentment and suspicion. What if the masses started following these teachings? Would the shells of the old ways be broken? If the multitude saw within themselves that which this renegade promised it would cause a catastrophe! Hospitals might be emptied! How would the children be taught? What would happen to the churches, social agencies, industries, and armies?

The whole system is founded on stirring up wants, needs, problems, poverty, strife and competition. A little trust in God, love, and peace is allright but not to the extent that it disrupts civilization.

And so the resistance mounted and organized. Only this time Solo was undaunted. He directed his People: "You know now the power of the words given to you many years ago. I came only to reveal their meanings. Go now into the world. Teach and live that others may know truth.

"Persevere so one day all may walk in the sun of perfect life."

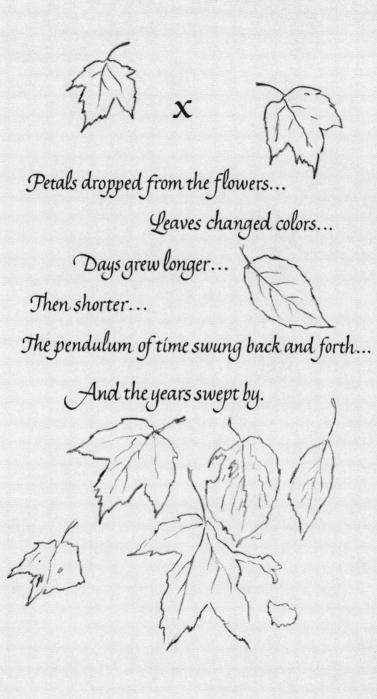

x

Petals dropped from the flowers...

Leaves changed colors...

Days grew longer...

Then shorter...

The pendulum of time swung back and forth...

And the years swept by.

There was some progress. But awareness is a transcendental substance that is written with a slow and faltering hand in the annals of time.

Perhaps humanity is never really ready for another step. It was difficult to distinguish that Solo was not talking about something new but, rather, something very old. Change was not being suggested but, instead, that which was changeless. Why is it so hard for mortals to look beyond themselves and understand what has been resting in the folds of civilization for ageless years? How long before such things surpass all else in importance?

Like all elements of a transient quality, Solo's body became quite aged. The days of its lasting were few.

The seeds of his dreams had been planted. It was up to destiny to nurture them. Others would have to dream the dreams.

Still a part of the world, Solo was fond of walking by the sea, watching the birds and clouds in the sun and the stars and moon at night. The mind, in which he lived, was especially treasured. Although the body had lost some of its strength, the spirit had not. It became increasingly restless for a new adventure, to wander beyond what was previously known. What once loomed as a lonely departure was now sensed as a lovely return.

His existence had become quite hermit-like. Rarely did he have contact with others, even his own People. The scarcity of his words made them all the more precious. Villagers would gather to listen when he appeared on the streets.

On one such occasion Solo was sitting in the village square talking to a small group circling him.

Suddenly he arose. Words formed quietly. "I have but a short time now."

He looked into the sun and his body seemed surrounded by brightness.

"I am the light of your lives," he said, "and have come to tell you of the two greatest principles of life."

"First, I shall speak of your spirit, which is, in truth, your real nature. It is like a darting shadow which loses itself in the darkness of your mind. So you go to your buildings and books and wise ones seeking to know who you are and what you are to be. I ask you to look about you at all that grows...the trees, the birds, and the flowers. Do they need words or teachers to tell them what they are to become? Is their spirit so different from yours? If there is that within them that works such unknowing wonders then how much greater it can become in you who have been given the power of knowing yourselves.

"Next, look at one another. What do you see? Can you judge from what your eyes tell you? Do you know the taste of the fruit by looking at it? Can you sense the fragrance of the flower without coming close to it? If the flowers of the field and fruits of the tree hold within them such pleasure for you what larger measure of joy is resting unseen in the most perfect of all creations...those about you? Know each other that you may find the meaning of love.

"If you have heard my words then speak of them according to your understanding."

With that Solo turned and walked into the sunshine leaving the people behind to wonder at his wisdom.

XI

Those were to be his last teachings.

For they found him a few days later sitting by
the seashore, gazing far away. He did not
speak and appeared unable to walk. No one
knew how long he had been there.

He was taken away with blinking lights and a screeching siren to a big building filled with little rooms and long hallways where people dressed in white were scurrying to and fro. Needles and pills were put into him.

His consciousness was dulled with chemicals and Solo lost the use of that which was cherished most. His mind.

At last the opulent spirit was quelled. The drugs made him one of them. Their wills could be imposed upon him.

Time lingered on. It hobbled along so slowly. Oh, to be free again!

And then one night Solo awoke. Outside was darkness. But the room was filled with soft light. Then it grew brighter gradually changing into beams of sun quivering through leaves of trees gilding a meadow of green grass and purple clover.

In the distance was a man who started walking closer. The sunshine seemed to surround the strong graceful figure clothed in a sheath of white. He moved through trees, then across the field until Solo could see the long hair.... the tanned skin...the beard...and a familiar kind face with gentle eyes.

The man spoke. "You did all you could, Solo. They will know us better in time."

There was tenderness and compassion in the voice. The mouth showed a faint smile.

"Come now, my friend. The things that you have been seeking are waiting."

Solo stood and walked across the meadow...
through the flowers...under the trees. There
was sunshine and blue. And presently the
mountains and the sea.

Finally the illusion of the mind had become
the reality of the spirit.

At last he knew...

As he had also been known.